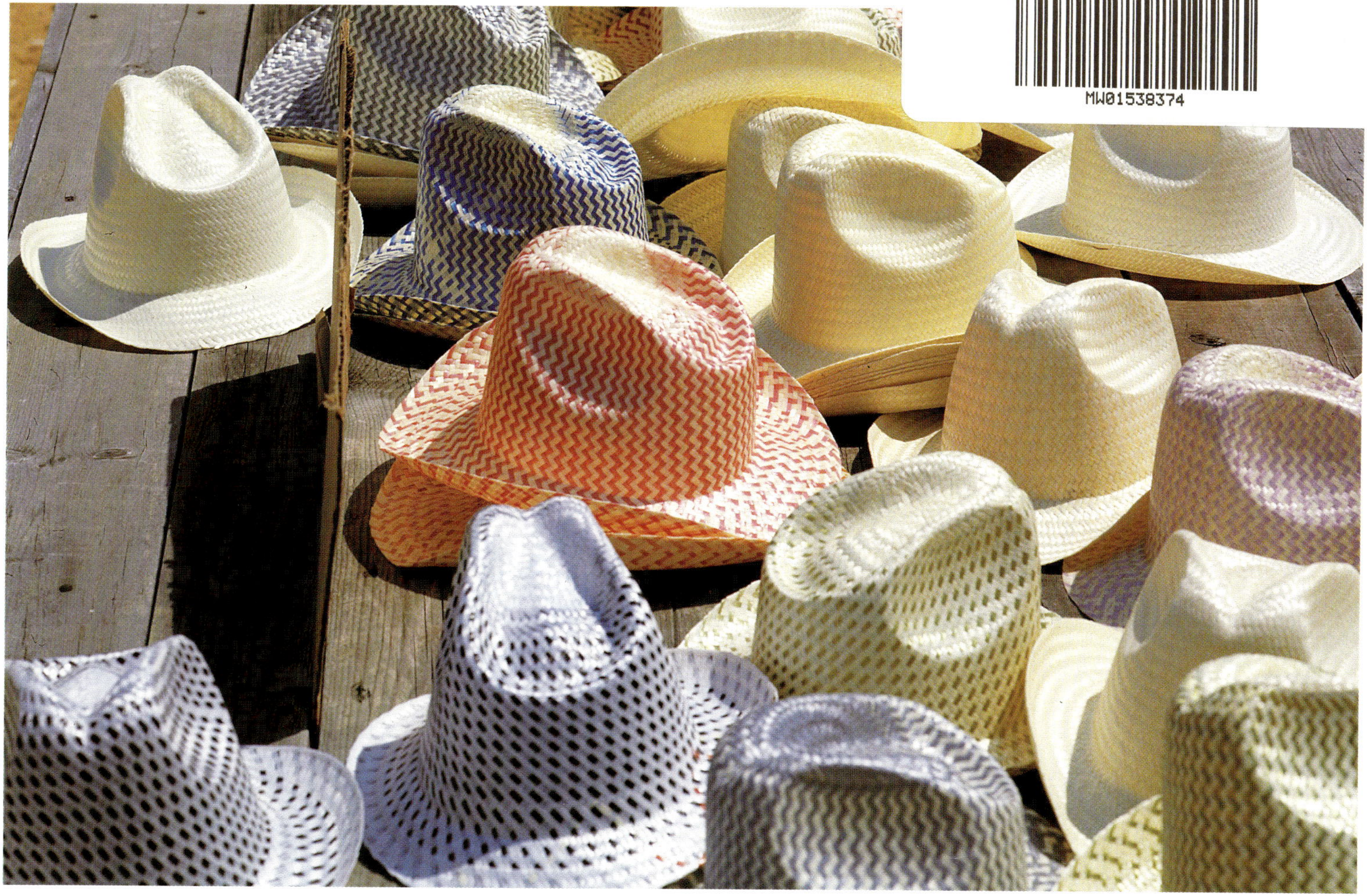

hats

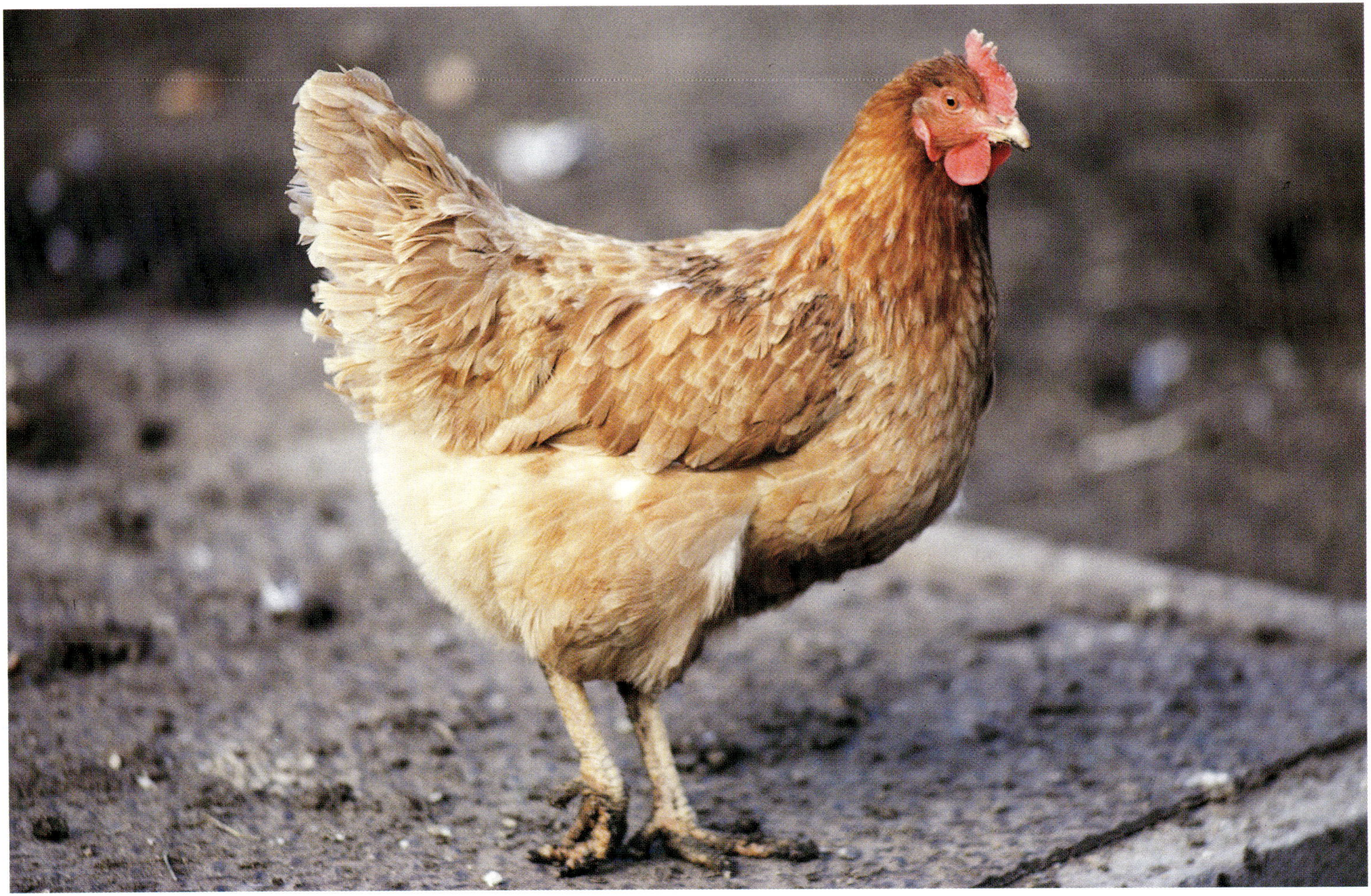

hen

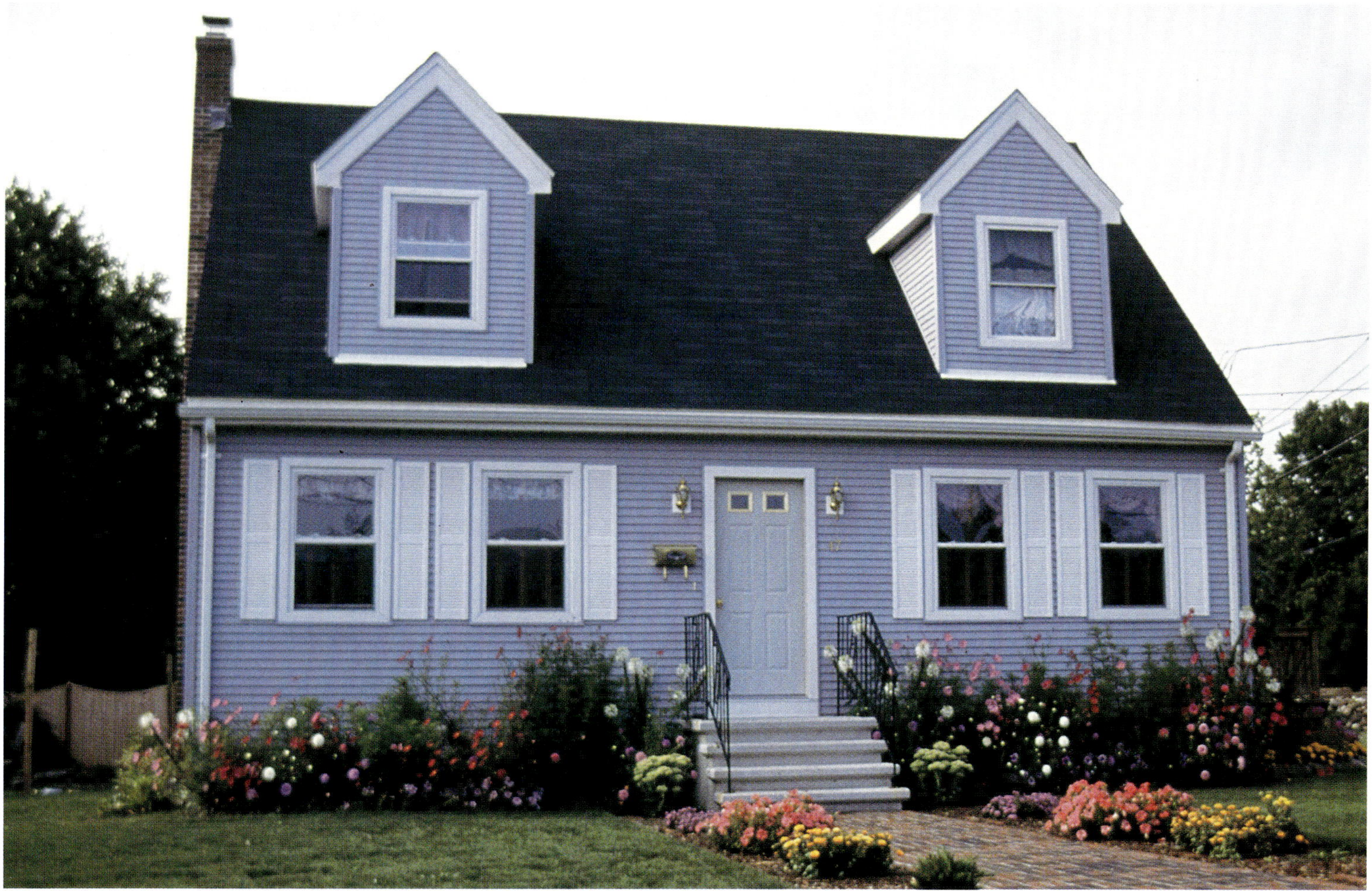

house

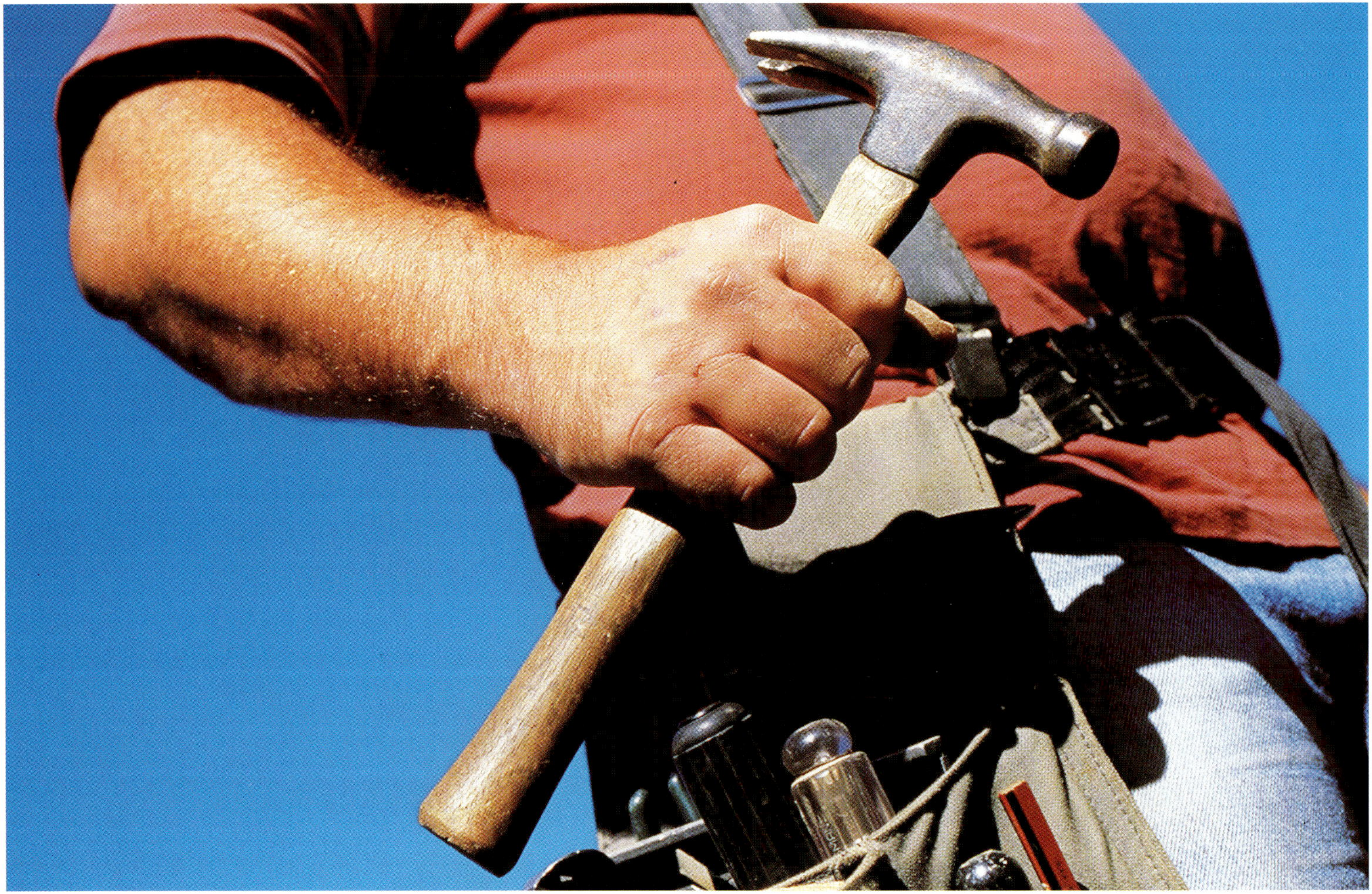

hammer

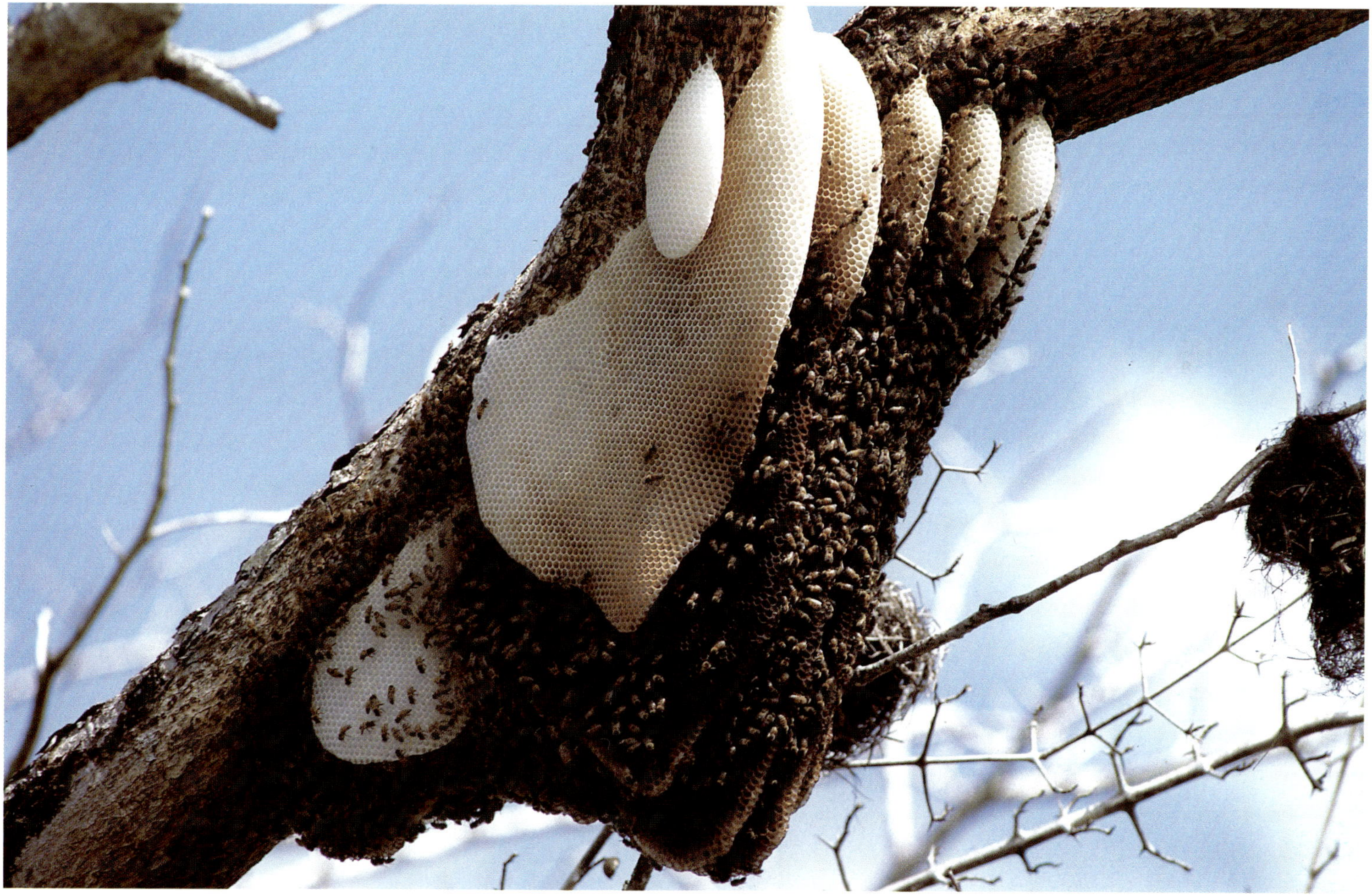

hive

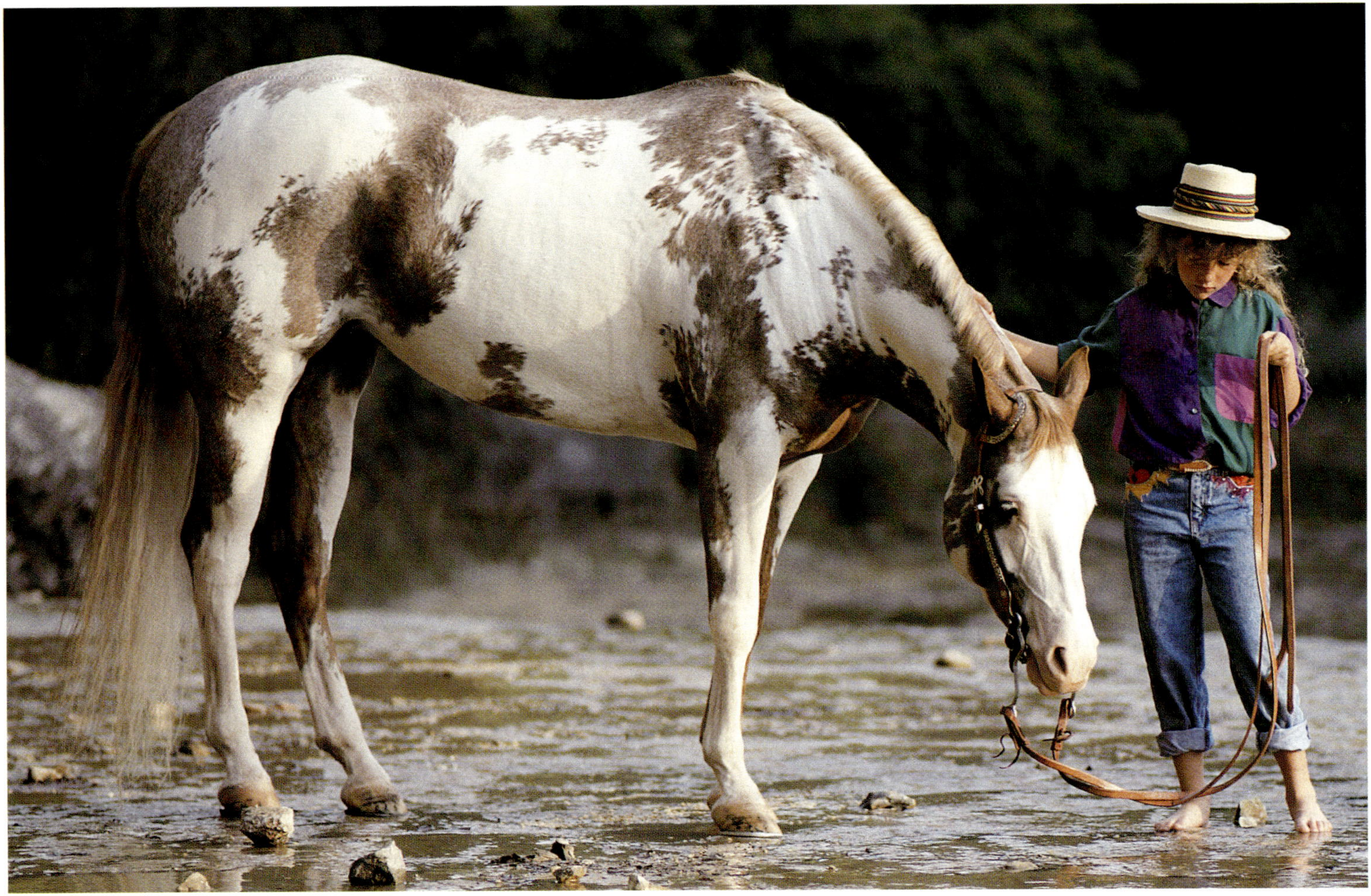

horse

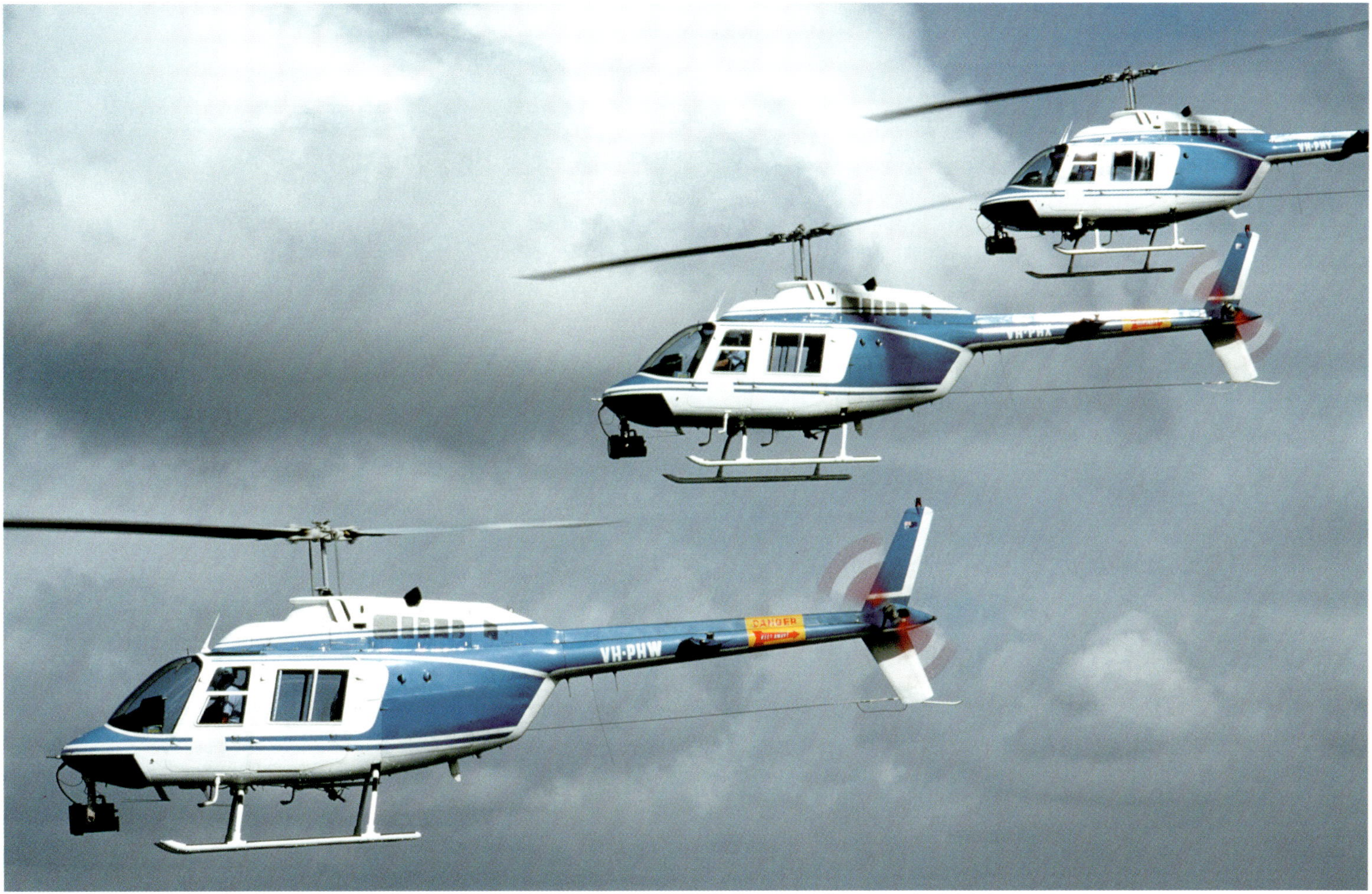

helicopters

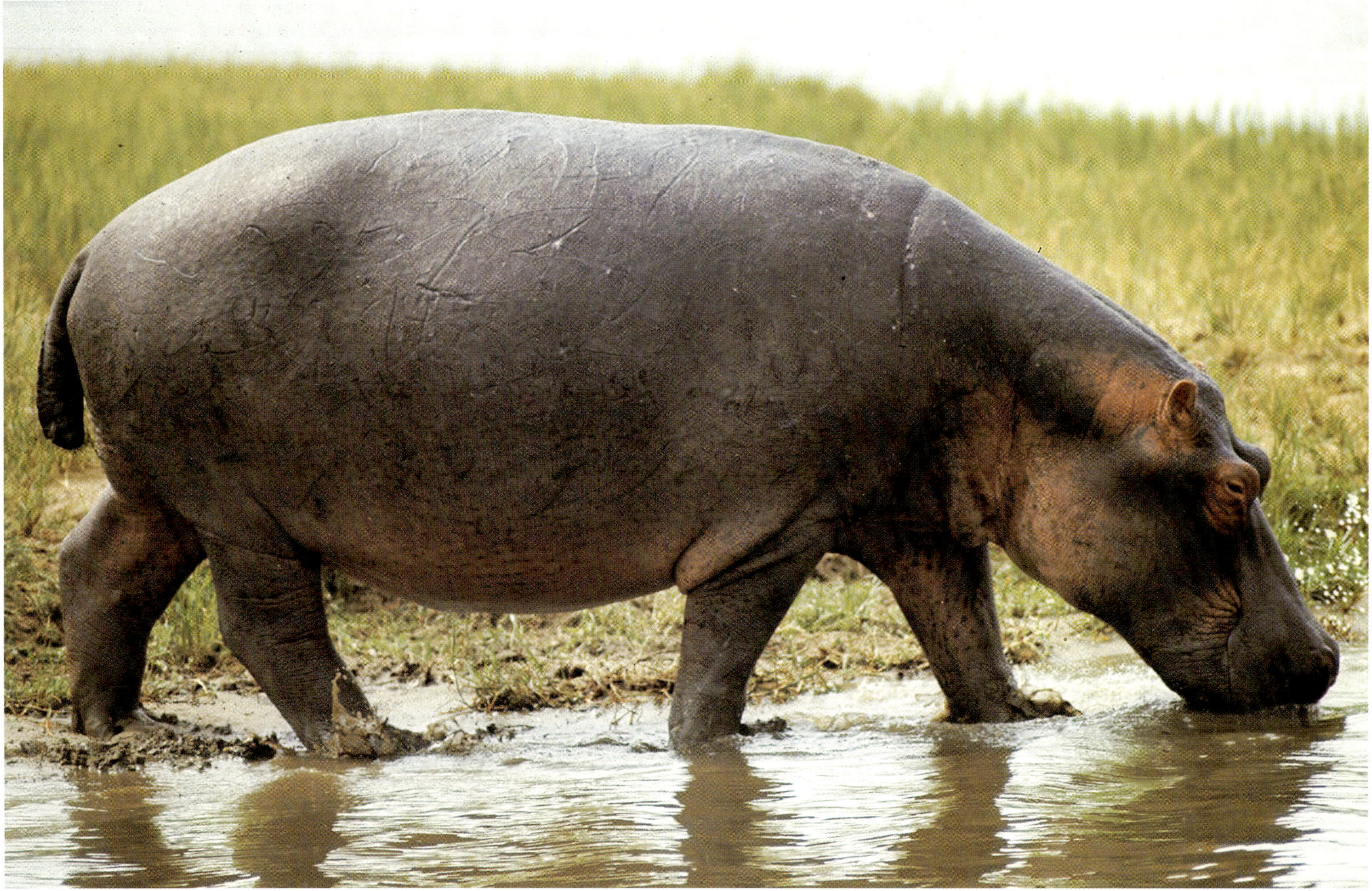

hippopotamus